THIS TEACHER PLANNER BELONGS TO:

_____

TEACHER *Information*

CLASS #: _____ SCHOOL: _____
GRADE: _____ ADDRESS: _____
SCHOOL YEAR: _____ PHONE: _____

NOTES & MEMOS

RESOURCE LINKS

PERSONAL NOTES

SCHOOL *Holidays*

AUGUST

SEPTEMBER

OCTOBER

NOVEMBER

DECEMBER

NOTES

SCHOOL *Holidays*

JANUARY	FEBRUARY	MARCH

APRIL	MAY	JUNE

NOTES:

YEAR AT A *Glance*

AUGUST	SEPTEMBER	OCTOBER

NOVEMBER	DECEMBER	JANUARY

FEBRUARY	MARCH	APRIL

MAY	JUNE

NOTES:

PARENT *Contacts*

STUDENT:	STUDENT:
PARENTS:	PARENTS:
PHONE #:	PHONE #:
EMAIL:	EMAIL:
STUDENT:	STUDENT:
PARENTS:	PARENTS:
PHONE #:	PHONE #:
EMAIL:	EMAIL:
STUDENT:	STUDENT:
PARENTS:	PARENTS:
PHONE #:	PHONE #:
EMAIL:	EMAIL:
STUDENT:	STUDENT:
PARENTS:	PARENTS:
PHONE #:	PHONE #:
EMAIL:	EMAIL:
STUDENT:	STUDENT:
PARENTS:	PARENTS:
PHONE #:	PHONE #:
EMAIL:	EMAIL:

PARENT Contacts

STUDENT: _____
PARENTS: _____
PHONE #: _____
EMAIL: _____

STUDENT: _____
PARENTS: _____
PHONE #: _____
EMAIL: _____

STUDENT: _____
PARENTS: _____
PHONE #: _____
EMAIL: _____

STUDENT: _____
PARENTS: _____
PHONE #: _____
EMAIL: _____

STUDENT: _____
PARENTS: _____
PHONE #: _____
EMAIL: _____

STUDENT: _____
PARENTS: _____
PHONE #: _____
EMAIL: _____

STUDENT: _____
PARENTS: _____
PHONE #: _____
EMAIL: _____

STUDENT: _____
PARENTS: _____
PHONE #: _____
EMAIL: _____

STUDENT: _____
PARENTS: _____
PHONE #: _____
EMAIL: _____

STUDENT: _____
PARENTS: _____
PHONE #: _____
EMAIL: _____

PARENT Contacts

STUDENT:	STUDENT:
PARENTS:	PARENTS:
PHONE #:	PHONE #:
EMAIL:	EMAIL:

STUDENT:	STUDENT:
PARENTS:	PARENTS:
PHONE #:	PHONE #:
EMAIL:	EMAIL:

STUDENT:	STUDENT:
PARENTS:	PARENTS:
PHONE #:	PHONE #:
EMAIL:	EMAIL:

STUDENT:	STUDENT:
PARENTS:	PARENTS:
PHONE #:	PHONE #:
EMAIL:	EMAIL:

STUDENT:	STUDENT:
PARENTS:	PARENTS:
PHONE #:	PHONE #:
EMAIL:	EMAIL:

PARENT CONTACT *Log*

MONTH:

NAME & DATE: **REASON:** **METHOD:** **NOTES:**
- EMAIL:
- PHONE:
- MEETING:

DATE: **REASON:** **METHOD:** **NOTES:**
- EMAIL:
- PHONE:
- MEETING:

DATE: **REASON:** **METHOD:** **NOTES:**
- EMAIL:
- PHONE:
- MEETING:

DATE: **REASON:** **METHOD:** **NOTES:**
- EMAIL:
- PHONE:
- MEETING:

DATE: **REASON:** **METHOD:** **NOTES:**
- EMAIL:
- PHONE:
- MEETING:

NOTES

PARENT CONTACT *Log*

MONTH:

NAME & DATE:	REASON:	METHOD:		NOTES:
		EMAIL:	☐	
		PHONE:	☐	
		MEETING:	☐	

DATE:	REASON:	METHOD:		NOTES:
		EMAIL:	☐	
		PHONE:	☐	
		MEETING:	☐	

DATE:	REASON:	METHOD:		NOTES:
		EMAIL:	☐	
		PHONE:	☐	
		MEETING:	☐	

DATE:	REASON:	METHOD:		NOTES:
		EMAIL:	☐	
		PHONE:	☐	
		MEETING:	☐	

DATE:	REASON:	METHOD:		NOTES:
		EMAIL:	☐	
		PHONE:	☐	
		MEETING:	☐	

NOTES

PARENT CONTACT *Log*

MONTH:

NAME & DATE:	**REASON:**	**METHOD:**	**NOTES:**
		EMAIL: ☐ PHONE: ☐ MEETING: ☐	

DATE:	**REASON:**	**METHOD:**	**NOTES:**
		EMAIL: ☐ PHONE: ☐ MEETING: ☐	

DATE:	**REASON:**	**METHOD:**	**NOTES:**
		EMAIL: ☐ PHONE: ☐ MEETING: ☐	

DATE:	**REASON:**	**METHOD:**	**NOTES:**
		EMAIL: ☐ PHONE: ☐ MEETING: ☐	

DATE:	**REASON:**	**METHOD:**	**NOTES:**
		EMAIL: ☐ PHONE: ☐ MEETING: ☐	

NOTES

PARENT CONTACT *Log*

MONTH:

NAME & DATE:	REASON:	METHOD:		NOTES:
		EMAIL:	☐	
		PHONE:	☐	
		MEETING:	☐	

DATE:	REASON:	METHOD:		NOTES:
		EMAIL:	☐	
		PHONE:	☐	
		MEETING:	☐	

DATE:	REASON:	METHOD:		NOTES:
		EMAIL:	☐	
		PHONE:	☐	
		MEETING:	☐	

DATE:	REASON:	METHOD:		NOTES:
		EMAIL:	☐	
		PHONE:	☐	
		MEETING:	☐	

DATE:	REASON:	METHOD:		NOTES:
		EMAIL:	☐	
		PHONE:	☐	
		MEETING:	☐	

NOTES

PARENT CONTACT *Log*

MONTH:

NAME & DATE:	REASON:	METHOD:	NOTES:
		EMAIL:	
		PHONE:	
		MEETING:	

DATE:	REASON:	METHOD:	NOTES:
		EMAIL:	
		PHONE:	
		MEETING:	

DATE:	REASON:	METHOD:	NOTES:
		EMAIL:	
		PHONE:	
		MEETING:	

DATE:	REASON:	METHOD:	NOTES:
		EMAIL:	
		PHONE:	
		MEETING:	

DATE:	REASON:	METHOD:	NOTES:
		EMAIL:	
		PHONE:	
		MEETING:	

NOTES

PARENT CONTACT *Log*

MONTH:

NAME & DATE:	REASON:	METHOD:	NOTES:
		EMAIL: ☐	
		PHONE: ☐	
		MEETING: ☐	

DATE:	REASON:	METHOD:	NOTES:
		EMAIL: ☐	
		PHONE: ☐	
		MEETING: ☐	

DATE:	REASON:	METHOD:	NOTES:
		EMAIL: ☐	
		PHONE: ☐	
		MEETING: ☐	

DATE:	REASON:	METHOD:	NOTES:
		EMAIL: ☐	
		PHONE: ☐	
		MEETING: ☐	

DATE:	REASON:	METHOD:	NOTES:
		EMAIL: ☐	
		PHONE: ☐	
		MEETING: ☐	

NOTES

STUDENT *Birthdays*

AUGUST

SEPTEMBER

OCTOBER

NOVEMBER

DECEMBER

JANUARY

FEBRUARY

MARCH

APRIL

MAY

JUNE

CLASSROOM *Expenses*

MONTH: _____   **YEAR:** _____

CLASS: _____

DATE	ITEM	DESCRIPTION	CATEGORY	COST

DATE:

CLASS Field Trip

EVENT

DATE:

LOCATION

TIME

DEPT TIME:

TOTAL COST:

RETURN TIME:

CONTACT

FIELD TRIP Checklist

IMPORTANT Reminders

Field Trip Itinerary

TIME:	ACTIVITIES:

PROGRESS *Report*

CLASS/SUBJECT:

DATE	SUBJECT/CLASS	LESSON PLAN #	ASSIGNMENTS

NOTES & IDEAS

ASSESSMENT

CUSTOMIZED ACTION PLAN

ASSIGNMENT *Tracker*

CLASS/SUBJECT: _____ WEEK OF: _____

MONDAY:	TUESDAY	WEDNESDAY

THURSDAY	FRIDAY	NOTES:

READING *Tracker*

CLASS: ....

BOOK TITLE: **AUTHOR:**

DATE	STUDENT	PAGES READ	NOTES

MONTHLY *Notes*

AUGUST

M	T	W	T	F

NOTES, ACTIVITIES, PLANS & IDEAS

MONTHLY *Schedule*

CLASSROOM: **MONTH:**

M	T	W	T	F	S	S

NOTES, ACTIVITIES, PLANS & IDEAS

MONTHLY *Notes*

	SEPTEMBER				
	M	T	W	T	F

NOTES, ACTIVITIES, PLANS & IDEAS

MONTHLY Schedule

CLASSROOM: **MONTH:**

M	T	W	T	F	S	S

NOTES, ACTIVITIES, PLANS & IDEAS

MONTHLY Notes

OCTOBER				
M	T	W	T	F

NOTES, ACTIVITIES, PLANS & IDEAS

MONTHLY *Schedule*

CLASSROOM: **MONTH:**

M	T	W	T	F	S	S

NOTES, ACTIVITIES, PLANS & IDEAS

MONTHLY *Notes*

	NOVEMBER				
M	T	W	T	F	

NOTES, ACTIVITIES, PLANS & IDEAS

MONTHLY *Schedule*

CLASSROOM: **MONTH:**

M	T	W	T	F	S	S

NOTES, ACTIVITIES, PLANS & IDEAS

MONTHLY Notes

DECEMBER

M	T	W	T	F

NOTES, ACTIVITIES, PLANS & IDEAS

MONTHLY Schedule

CLASSROOM: **MONTH:**

M	T	W	T	F	S	S

NOTES, ACTIVITIES, PLANS & IDEAS

MONTHLY Notes

JANUARY

M	T	W	T	F

NOTES, ACTIVITIES, PLANS & IDEAS

MONTHLY Schedule

CLASSROOM: **MONTH:**

M	T	W	T	F	S	S

NOTES, ACTIVITIES, PLANS & IDEAS

MONTHLY *Notes*

FEBRUARY

M	T	W	T	F

NOTES, ACTIVITIES, PLANS & IDEAS

MONTHLY Schedule

CLASSROOM: **MONTH:**

M	T	W	T	F	S	S

NOTES, ACTIVITIES, PLANS & IDEAS

MONTHLY *Notes*

MARCH				
M	T	W	T	F

NOTES, ACTIVITIES, PLANS & IDEAS

MONTHLY *Schedule*

CLASSROOM: **MONTH:**

M	T	W	T	F	S	S

NOTES, ACTIVITIES, PLANS & IDEAS

MONTHLY *Notes*

APRIL

M	T	W	T	F

NOTES, ACTIVITIES, PLANS & IDEAS

MONTHLY Schedule

CLASSROOM: **MONTH:**

M	T	W	T	F	S	S

NOTES, ACTIVITIES, PLANS & IDEAS

MONTHLY *Notes*

MAY

M	T	W	T	F

NOTES, ACTIVITIES, PLANS & IDEAS

MONTHLY *Schedule*

CLASSROOM: **MONTH:**

M	T	W	T	F	S	S

NOTES, ACTIVITIES, PLANS & IDEAS

MONTHLY Notes

	JUNE			
M	T	W	T	F

NOTES, ACTIVITIES, PLANS & IDEAS

MONTHLY Schedule

CLASSROOM: **MONTH:**

M	T	W	T	F	S	S

NOTES, ACTIVITIES, PLANS & IDEAS

DATE:

WEEKLY ROLL *Call*

FIRST NAME: LAST NAME: STATUS:

WEEKLY *Overview*

WEEK OF: ....

MONDAY

TUESDAY

WEDNESDAY

THURSDAY

FRIDAY

SATURDAY

SUNDAY

IMPORTANT NOTES

WEEKLY Lesson Plan

MONDAY

EQ/ I CAN NOTES:

TUESDAY

EQ/ I CAN NOTES:

WEDNESDAY

EQ/ I CAN NOTES:

THURSDAY

EQ/ I CAN NOTES:

FRIDAY

EQ/ I CAN NOTES:

CLASS Projects

PROJECT TITLE:

DETAILS:

START DATE:

DUE DATE:

DATE	TASK COMPLETED

READING *Tracker*

CLASS: _____

BOOK TITLE: _____ **AUTHOR:** _____

DATE	STUDENT	PAGES READ	NOTES

WEEKLY *Planner*

MONDAY

TUESDAY

WEDNESDAY

THURSDAY

FRIDAY

EQ/I CAN NOTES:

LESSON Planner

SUBJECT:

UNIT:

LESSON:

DATE:

OBJECTIVE:

OVERVIEW

TOPICS COVERED

ASSIGNMENTS

NOTES

ASSIGNMENT *Tracker*

CLASS/SUBJECT: —————————————— WEEK OF: ——————————————

MONDAY:	TUESDAY	WEDNESDAY

THURSDAY	FRIDAY	NOTES:

DAILY Schedule

TO DO LIST: **DATE**

Time
6 AM
7 AM
8 AM
9 AM
10 AM
11 AM
12 PM
1 PM
2 PM
3 PM
4 PM
5 PM
6 PM
7 PM
8 PM
9 PM
10 PM

REMINDERS:

NOTES:

NOTES

DAY PLANNER *Monday*

DATE:

5am:

6am:

7am:

8am:

9am:

10am:

11am:

12pm:

1pm:

2pm:

3pm:

4pm:

DAILY TO DO LIST:

DAILY GOALS:

NOTES & REMINDERS:

DAY PLANNER

DATE:

5am:

6am:

7am:

8am:

9am:

10am:

11am:

12pm:

1pm:

2pm:

3pm:

4pm:

DAILY TO DO LIST:

DAILY GOALS:

NOTES & REMINDERS:

DAY PLANNER *Wednesday*

DATE:

5am:

6am:

7am:

8am:

9am:

10am:

11am:

12pm:

1pm:

2pm:

3pm:

4pm:

DAILY TO DO LIST:

DAILY GOALS:

NOTES & REMINDERS:

DAY PLANNER *Thursday*

DATE:

5am:

6am:

7am:

8am:

9am:

10am:

11am:

12pm:

1pm:

2pm:

3pm:

4pm:

DAILY TO DO LIST:

DAILY GOALS:

NOTES & REMINDERS:

DAY PLANNER *Friday*

DATE:

5am:

6am:

7am:

8am:

9am:

10am:

11am:

12pm:

1pm:

2pm:

3pm:

4pm:

DAILY TO DO LIST:

DAILY GOALS:

NOTES & REMINDERS:

DATE:

WEEKLY ROLL Call

FIRST NAME: LAST NAME: STATUS:

WEEKLY *Overview*

WEEK OF: _____

MONDAY

TUESDAY

WEDNESDAY

THURSDAY

FRIDAY

SATURDAY

SUNDAY

IMPORTANT NOTES

WEEKLY Lesson Plan

MONDAY

EQ/ I CAN NOTES:

TUESDAY

EQ/ I CAN NOTES:

WEDNESDAY

EQ/ I CAN NOTES:

THURSDAY

EQ/ I CAN NOTES:

FRIDAY

EQ/ I CAN NOTES:

READING *Tracker*

CLASS: _____

BOOK TITLE: _____ **AUTHOR:** _____

DATE	STUDENT	PAGES READ	NOTES

LESSON Planner

SUBJECT:

UNIT:

LESSON:

DATE:

OBJECTIVE:

OVERVIEW

TOPICS COVERED

ASSIGNMENTS

NOTES

DAY PLANNER *Monday*

DATE:

5am:

6am:

7am:

8am:

9am:

10am:

11am:

12pm:

1pm:

2pm:

3pm:

4pm:

DAILY TO DO LIST:

DAILY GOALS:

NOTES & REMINDERS:

DAY PLANNER

DATE:

5am:

6am:

7am:

8am:

9am:

10am:

11am:

12pm:

1pm:

2pm:

3pm:

4pm:

DAILY TO DO LIST:

DAILY GOALS:

NOTES & REMINDERS:

DAY PLANNER *Wednesday*

DATE:

5am:

6am:

7am:

8am:

9am:

10am:

11am:

12pm:

1pm:

2pm:

3pm:

4pm:

DAILY TO DO LIST:

DAILY GOALS:

NOTES & REMINDERS:

DAY PLANNER *Thursday*

DATE:

5am:

6am:

7am:

8am:

9am:

10am:

11am:

12pm:

1pm:

2pm:

3pm:

4pm:

DAILY TO DO LIST:

DAILY GOALS:

NOTES & REMINDERS:

DAY PLANNER *Friday*

DATE:

5am:

6am:

7am:

8am:

9am:

10am:

11am:

12pm:

1pm:

2pm:

3pm:

4pm:

DAILY TO DO LIST:

DAILY GOALS:

NOTES & REMINDERS:

DATE:

WEEKLY ROLL *Call*

FIRST NAME: LAST NAME: STATUS:

WEEKLY Overview

WEEK OF: ....

MONDAY

TUESDAY

WEDNESDAY

THURSDAY

FRIDAY

SATURDAY

SUNDAY

IMPORTANT NOTES

WEEKLY Lesson Plan

MONDAY

EQ/ I CAN NOTES:

TUESDAY

EQ/ I CAN NOTES:

WEDNESDAY

EQ/ I CAN NOTES:

THURSDAY

EQ/ I CAN NOTES:

FRIDAY

EQ/ I CAN NOTES:

READING *Tracker*

CLASS: _____

BOOK TITLE: _____ **AUTHOR:** _____

DATE	STUDENT	PAGES READ	NOTES

LESSON *Planner*

SUBJECT:

UNIT:

LESSON:

DATE:

OBJECTIVE:

OVERVIEW

TOPICS COVERED

ASSIGNMENTS

NOTES

DAY PLANNER *Monday*

DATE:

5am:

6am:

7am:

8am:

9am:

10am:

11am:

12pm:

1pm:

2pm:

3pm:

4pm:

DAILY TO DO LIST:

DAILY GOALS:

NOTES & REMINDERS:

DAY PLANNER

DATE:

5am:

6am:

7am:

8am:

9am:

10am:

11am:

12pm:

1pm:

2pm:

3pm:

4pm:

DAILY TO DO LIST:

DAILY GOALS:

NOTES & REMINDERS:

DAY PLANNER *Wednesday*

DATE:

5am:

6am:

7am:

8am:

9am:

10am:

11am:

12pm:

1pm:

2pm:

3pm:

4pm:

DAILY TO DO LIST:

DAILY GOALS:

NOTES & REMINDERS:

DAY PLANNER *Thursday*

DATE:

5am:

6am:

7am:

8am:

9am:

10am:

11am:

12pm:

1pm:

2pm:

3pm:

4pm:

DAILY TO DO LIST:

DAILY GOALS:

NOTES & REMINDERS:

DAY PLANNER — Friday

DATE:

5am:

6am:

7am:

8am:

9am:

10am:

11am:

12pm:

1pm:

2pm:

3pm:

4pm:

DAILY TO DO LIST:

DAILY GOALS:

NOTES & REMINDERS:

DATE:

WEEKLY ROLL *Call*

FIRST NAME: LAST NAME: STATUS:

WEEKLY *Overview*

WEEK OF: ....

MONDAY

TUESDAY

WEDNESDAY

THURSDAY

FRIDAY

SATURDAY

SUNDAY

IMPORTANT NOTES

WEEKLY Lesson Plan

MONDAY

EQ/ I CAN NOTES:

TUESDAY

EQ/ I CAN NOTES:

WEDNESDAY

EQ/ I CAN NOTES:

THURSDAY

EQ/ I CAN NOTES:

FRIDAY

EQ/ I CAN NOTES:

READING Tracker

CLASS: _____

BOOK TITLE: _____ **AUTHOR:** _____

DATE	STUDENT	PAGES READ	NOTES

LESSON *Planner*

SUBJECT:

UNIT:

LESSON:

DATE:

OBJECTIVE:

OVERVIEW

TOPICS COVERED

ASSIGNMENTS

NOTES

DAY PLANNER *Monday*

DATE:

5am:

6am:

7am:

8am:

9am:

10am:

11am:

12pm:

1pm:

2pm:

3pm:

4pm:

DAILY TO DO LIST:

DAILY GOALS:

NOTES & REMINDERS:

DAY PLANNER

DATE:

5am:

6am:

7am:

8am:

9am:

10am:

11am:

12pm:

1pm:

2pm:

3pm:

4pm:

DAILY TO DO LIST:

DAILY GOALS:

NOTES & REMINDERS:

DAY PLANNER *Wednesday*

DATE:

5am:

6am:

7am:

8am:

9am:

10am:

11am:

12pm:

1pm:

2pm:

3pm:

4pm:

DAILY TO DO LIST:

DAILY GOALS:

NOTES & REMINDERS:

DAY PLANNER *Thursday*

DATE:

5am:

6am:

7am:

8am:

9am:

10am:

11am:

12pm:

1pm:

2pm:

3pm:

4pm:

DAILY TO DO LIST:

DAILY GOALS:

NOTES & REMINDERS:

DAY PLANNER — Friday

DATE:

5am:

6am:

7am:

8am:

9am:

10am:

11am:

12pm:

1pm:

2pm:

3pm:

4pm:

DAILY TO DO LIST:

DAILY GOALS:

NOTES & REMINDERS:

DATE: _____

WEEKLY ROLL *Call*

FIRST NAME:	LAST NAME:	STATUS:

WEEKLY *Overview*

WEEK OF: _____

MONDAY

TUESDAY

WEDNESDAY

THURSDAY

FRIDAY

SATURDAY

SUNDAY

IMPORTANT NOTES

WEEKLY Lesson Plan

MONDAY

EQ/ I CAN NOTES:

TUESDAY

EQ/ I CAN NOTES:

WEDNESDAY

EQ/ I CAN NOTES:

THURSDAY

EQ/ I CAN NOTES:

FRIDAY

EQ/ I CAN NOTES:

READING Tracker

CLASS:

BOOK TITLE: **AUTHOR:**

DATE	STUDENT	PAGES READ	NOTES

LESSON *Planner*

SUBJECT:

UNIT:

LESSON:

DATE:

OBJECTIVE:

OVERVIEW

TOPICS COVERED

ASSIGNMENTS

NOTES

DAY PLANNER *Monday*

DATE:

5am:

6am:

7am:

8am:

9am:

10am:

11am:

12pm:

1pm:

2pm:

3pm:

4pm:

DAILY TO DO LIST:

DAILY GOALS:

NOTES & REMINDERS:

DAY PLANNER — Tuesday

DATE:

5am:

6am:

7am:

8am:

9am:

10am:

11am:

12pm:

1pm:

2pm:

3pm:

4pm:

DAILY TO DO LIST:

DAILY GOALS:

NOTES & REMINDERS:

DAY PLANNER — Wednesday

DATE:

5am:

6am:

7am:

8am:

9am:

10am:

11am:

12pm:

1pm:

2pm:

3pm:

4pm:

DAILY TO DO LIST:

DAILY GOALS:

NOTES & REMINDERS:

DAY PLANNER *Thursday*

DATE:

5am:

6am:

7am:

8am:

9am:

10am:

11am:

12pm:

1pm:

2pm:

3pm:

4pm:

DAILY TO DO LIST:

DAILY GOALS:

NOTES & REMINDERS:

DAY PLANNER *Friday*

DATE:

5am:

6am:

7am:

8am:

9am:

10am:

11am:

12pm:

1pm:

2pm:

3pm:

4pm:

DAILY TO DO LIST:

DAILY GOALS:

NOTES & REMINDERS:

DATE:

WEEKLY ROLL *Call*

FIRST NAME:	LAST NAME:	STATUS:

WEEKLY *Overview*

WEEK OF: ....

MONDAY

TUESDAY

WEDNESDAY

THURSDAY

FRIDAY

SATURDAY

SUNDAY

IMPORTANT NOTES

WEEKLY Lesson Plan

MONDAY

EQ/ I CAN NOTES:

TUESDAY

EQ/ I CAN NOTES:

WEDNESDAY

EQ/ I CAN NOTES:

THURSDAY

EQ/ I CAN NOTES:

FRIDAY

EQ/ I CAN NOTES:

READING Tracker

CLASS: _____

BOOK TITLE:		AUTHOR:	
DATE	STUDENT	PAGES READ	NOTES

LESSON *Planner*

SUBJECT:

UNIT:

LESSON:

DATE:

OBJECTIVE:

OVERVIEW

TOPICS COVERED

ASSIGNMENTS

NOTES

DAY PLANNER *Monday*

DATE:

5am:

6am:

7am:

8am:

9am:

10am:

11am:

12pm:

1pm:

2pm:

3pm:

4pm:

DAILY TO DO LIST:

DAILY GOALS:

NOTES & REMINDERS:

DAY PLANNER

DATE:

5am:

6am:

7am:

8am:

9am:

10am:

11am:

12pm:

1pm:

2pm:

3pm:

4pm:

DAILY TO DO LIST:

DAILY GOALS:

NOTES & REMINDERS:

DAY PLANNER *Wednesday*

DATE:

5am:

6am:

7am:

8am:

9am:

10am:

11am:

12pm:

1pm:

2pm:

3pm:

4pm:

DAILY TO DO LIST:

DAILY GOALS:

NOTES & REMINDERS:

DAY PLANNER *Thursday*

DATE:

5am:

6am:

7am:

8am:

9am:

10am:

11am:

12pm:

1pm:

2pm:

3pm:

4pm:

DAILY TO DO LIST:

DAILY GOALS:

NOTES & REMINDERS:

DAY PLANNER *Friday*

DATE:

5am:

6am:

7am:

8am:

9am:

10am:

11am:

12pm:

1pm:

2pm:

3pm:

4pm:

DAILY TO DO LIST:

DAILY GOALS:

NOTES & REMINDERS:

DATE:

WEEKLY ROLL Call

FIRST NAME:	LAST NAME:	STATUS:

WEEKLY *Overview*

WEEK OF: ....

MONDAY

TUESDAY

WEDNESDAY

THURSDAY

FRIDAY

SATURDAY

SUNDAY

IMPORTANT NOTES

WEEKLY Lesson Plan

MONDAY

EQ/ I CAN NOTES:

TUESDAY

EQ/ I CAN NOTES:

WEDNESDAY

EQ/ I CAN NOTES:

THURSDAY

EQ/ I CAN NOTES:

FRIDAY

EQ/ I CAN NOTES:

READING Tracker

CLASS: _____

BOOK TITLE: _____ **AUTHOR:** _____

DATE	STUDENT	PAGES READ	NOTES

LESSON Planner

SUBJECT:

UNIT:

LESSON:

DATE:

OBJECTIVE:

OVERVIEW

TOPICS COVERED

ASSIGNMENTS

NOTES

DAY PLANNER *Monday*

DATE:

5am:

6am:

7am:

8am:

9am:

10am:

11am:

12pm:

1pm:

2pm:

3pm:

4pm:

DAILY TO DO LIST:

DAILY GOALS:

NOTES & REMINDERS:

DAY PLANNER

DATE:

5am:

6am:

7am:

8am:

9am:

10am:

11am:

12pm:

1pm:

2pm:

3pm:

4pm:

DAILY TO DO LIST:

DAILY GOALS:

NOTES & REMINDERS:

DAY PLANNER *Wednesday*

DATE:

5am:

6am:

7am:

8am:

9am:

10am:

11am:

12pm:

1pm:

2pm:

3pm:

4pm:

DAILY TO DO LIST:

DAILY GOALS:

NOTES & REMINDERS:

DAY PLANNER *Thursday*

DATE:

5am:

6am:

7am:

8am:

9am:

10am:

11am:

12pm:

1pm:

2pm:

3pm:

4pm:

DAILY TO DO LIST:

DAILY GOALS:

NOTES & REMINDERS:

DAY PLANNER *Friday*

DATE:

5am:

6am:

7am:

8am:

9am:

10am:

11am:

12pm:

1pm:

2pm:

3pm:

4pm:

DAILY TO DO LIST:

DAILY GOALS:

NOTES & REMINDERS:

DATE: _____

WEEKLY ROLL *Call*

FIRST NAME: LAST NAME: STATUS:

WEEKLY *Overview*

WEEK OF: ....

MONDAY

TUESDAY

WEDNESDAY

THURSDAY

FRIDAY

SATURDAY

SUNDAY

IMPORTANT NOTES

WEEKLY Lesson Plan

MONDAY

EQ/ I CAN NOTES:

TUESDAY

EQ/ I CAN NOTES:

WEDNESDAY

EQ/ I CAN NOTES:

THURSDAY

EQ/ I CAN NOTES:

FRIDAY

EQ/ I CAN NOTES:

READING Tracker

CLASS: _____

BOOK TITLE: _____ **AUTHOR:** _____

DATE	STUDENT	PAGES READ	NOTES

LESSON *Planner*

SUBJECT:

UNIT:

LESSON:

DATE:

OBJECTIVE:

OVERVIEW

TOPICS COVERED

ASSIGNMENTS

NOTES

DAY PLANNER *Monday*

DATE:

5am:

6am:

7am:

8am:

9am:

10am:

11am:

12pm:

1pm:

2pm:

3pm:

4pm:

DAILY TO DO LIST:

DAILY GOALS:

NOTES & REMINDERS:

DAY PLANNER

DATE:

5am:

6am:

7am:

8am:

9am:

10am:

11am:

12pm:

1pm:

2pm:

3pm:

4pm:

DAILY TO DO LIST:

DAILY GOALS:

NOTES & REMINDERS:

DAY PLANNER *Wednesday*

DATE:

5am:

6am:

7am:

8am:

9am:

10am:

11am:

12pm:

1pm:

2pm:

3pm:

4pm:

DAILY TO DO LIST:

DAILY GOALS:

NOTES & REMINDERS:

DAY PLANNER *Thursday*

DATE:

5am:

6am:

7am:

8am:

9am:

10am:

11am:

12pm:

1pm:

2pm:

3pm:

4pm:

DAILY TO DO LIST:

DAILY GOALS:

NOTES & REMINDERS:

DAY PLANNER *Friday*

DATE:

5am:

6am:

7am:

8am:

9am:

10am:

11am:

12pm:

1pm:

2pm:

3pm:

4pm:

DAILY TO DO LIST:

DAILY GOALS:

NOTES & REMINDERS:

DATE: _____

WEEKLY ROLL *Call*

FIRST NAME:	LAST NAME:	STATUS:

WEEKLY *Overview*

WEEK OF: ....

MONDAY

TUESDAY

WEDNESDAY

THURSDAY

FRIDAY

SATURDAY

SUNDAY

IMPORTANT NOTES

WEEKLY Lesson Plan

MONDAY

EQ/ I CAN NOTES:

TUESDAY

EQ/ I CAN NOTES:

WEDNESDAY

EQ/ I CAN NOTES:

THURSDAY

EQ/ I CAN NOTES:

FRIDAY

EQ/ I CAN NOTES:

READING Tracker

CLASS: _____

BOOK TITLE: **AUTHOR:**

DATE	STUDENT	PAGES READ	NOTES

LESSON *Planner*

SUBJECT:

UNIT:

LESSON:

DATE:

OBJECTIVE:

OVERVIEW

TOPICS COVERED

ASSIGNMENTS

NOTES

DAY PLANNER *Monday*

DATE:

5am:

6am:

7am:

8am:

9am:

10am:

11am:

12pm:

1pm:

2pm:

3pm:

4pm:

DAILY TO DO LIST:

DAILY GOALS:

NOTES & REMINDERS:

DAY PLANNER

DATE:

5am:

6am:

7am:

8am:

9am:

10am:

11am:

12pm:

1pm:

2pm:

3pm:

4pm:

DAILY TO DO LIST:

DAILY GOALS:

NOTES & REMINDERS:

DAY PLANNER *Wednesday*

DATE:

5am:

6am:

7am:

8am:

9am:

10am:

11am:

12pm:

1pm:

2pm:

3pm:

4pm:

DAILY TO DO LIST:

DAILY GOALS:

NOTES & REMINDERS:

DAY PLANNER *Thursday*

DATE:

5am:

6am:

7am:

8am:

9am:

10am:

11am:

12pm:

1pm:

2pm:

3pm:

4pm:

DAILY TO DO LIST:

DAILY GOALS:

NOTES & REMINDERS:

DAY PLANNER *Friday*

DATE:

5am:

6am:

7am:

8am:

9am:

10am:

11am:

12pm:

1pm:

2pm:

3pm:

4pm:

DAILY TO DO LIST:

DAILY GOALS:

NOTES & REMINDERS:

PARENT-TEACHER *Meetings*

STUDENT NAME:

DATE & TIME:

REASON FOR MEETING

TOPICS DISCUSSED	ACTION PLAN & GOALS

STUDENT NAME:

DATE & TIME:

REASON FOR MEETING

TOPICS DISCUSSED	ACTION PLAN & GOALS

STUDENT *Information*

STUDENT INFORMATION

NAME: _____ BIRTH DATE: _____
ADDRESS: _____ PARENTS NAMES: _____
PHONE: _____ EMAIL ADDRESS: _____

ACADEMIC HISTORY

STUDENT ID: _____
CHALLENGES: _____
STRENGTHS: _____

MEDICAL INFORMATION

_____
_____
_____

PRIMARY CONTACT INFORMATION

EMERGENCY CONTACT INFORMATION

ADDITIONAL INFORMATION

STUDENT *Information*

STUDENT INFORMATION

NAME: _____ BIRTH DATE: _____

ADDRESS: _____ PARENTS NAMES: _____

PHONE: _____ EMAIL ADDRESS: _____

ACADEMIC HISTORY

STUDENT ID: _____

CHALLENGES: _____

STRENGTHS: _____

MEDICAL INFORMATION

PRIMARY CONTACT INFORMATION

EMERGENCY CONTACT INFORMATION

ADDITIONAL INFORMATION

STUDENT *Information*

STUDENT INFORMATION

NAME: _____   BIRTH DATE: _____
ADDRESS: _____   PARENTS NAMES: _____
PHONE: _____   EMAIL ADDRESS: _____

ACADEMIC HISTORY

STUDENT ID: _____
CHALLENGES: _____
STRENGTHS: _____

MEDICAL INFORMATION

PRIMARY CONTACT INFORMATION

EMERGENCY CONTACT INFORMATION

ADDITIONAL INFORMATION

STUDENT Information

STUDENT INFORMATION

NAME: _____
ADDRESS: _____
PHONE: _____

BIRTH DATE: _____
PARENTS NAMES: _____
EMAIL ADDRESS: _____

ACADEMIC HISTORY

STUDENT ID: _____
CHALLENGES: _____
STRENGTHS: _____

MEDICAL INFORMATION

PRIMARY CONTACT INFORMATION

EMERGENCY CONTACT INFORMATION

ADDITIONAL INFORMATION

STUDENT *Information*

STUDENT INFORMATION

NAME: _____   BIRTH DATE: _____
ADDRESS: _____   PARENTS NAMES: _____
PHONE: _____   EMAIL ADDRESS: _____

ACADEMIC HISTORY

STUDENT ID: _____
CHALLENGES: _____
STRENGTHS: _____

MEDICAL INFORMATION

_____
_____
_____

PRIMARY CONTACT INFORMATION

EMERGENCY CONTACT INFORMATION

ADDITIONAL INFORMATION

STUDENT Information

STUDENT INFORMATION

NAME: _____ BIRTH DATE: _____

ADDRESS: _____ PARENTS NAMES: _____

PHONE: _____ EMAIL ADDRESS: _____

ACADEMIC HISTORY

STUDENT ID: _____

CHALLENGES: _____

STRENGTHS: _____

MEDICAL INFORMATION

PRIMARY CONTACT INFORMATION

EMERGENCY CONTACT INFORMATION

ADDITIONAL INFORMATION

STUDENT Information

STUDENT INFORMATION

NAME: _____ BIRTH DATE: _____
ADDRESS: _____ PARENTS NAMES: _____
PHONE: _____ EMAIL ADDRESS: _____

ACADEMIC HISTORY

STUDENT ID: _____
CHALLENGES: _____
STRENGTHS: _____

MEDICAL INFORMATION

_____
_____
_____

PRIMARY CONTACT INFORMATION

EMERGENCY CONTACT INFORMATION

ADDITIONAL INFORMATION

STUDENT *Information*

STUDENT INFORMATION

NAME: _____   BIRTH DATE: _____
ADDRESS: _____   PARENTS NAMES: _____
PHONE: _____   EMAIL ADDRESS: _____

ACADEMIC HISTORY

STUDENT ID: _____
CHALLENGES: _____
STRENGTHS: _____

MEDICAL INFORMATION

PRIMARY CONTACT INFORMATION

EMERGENCY CONTACT INFORMATION

ADDITIONAL INFORMATION

STUDENT *Information*

STUDENT INFORMATION

NAME: _____   BIRTH DATE: _____
ADDRESS: _____   PARENTS NAMES: _____
PHONE: _____   EMAIL ADDRESS: _____

ACADEMIC HISTORY

STUDENT ID: _____
CHALLENGES: _____
STRENGTHS: _____

MEDICAL INFORMATION

PRIMARY CONTACT INFORMATION

EMERGENCY CONTACT INFORMATION

ADDITIONAL INFORMATION

STUDENT *Information*

STUDENT INFORMATION

NAME: _____	BIRTH DATE: _____
ADDRESS: _____	PARENTS NAMES: _____
PHONE: _____	EMAIL ADDRESS: _____

ACADEMIC HISTORY

STUDENT ID: _____
CHALLENGES: _____
STRENGTHS: _____

MEDICAL INFORMATION

PRIMARY CONTACT INFORMATION

EMERGENCY CONTACT INFORMATION

ADDITIONAL INFORMATION

STUDENT *Information*

STUDENT INFORMATION

NAME: _____   BIRTH DATE: _____
ADDRESS: _____   PARENTS NAMES: _____
PHONE: _____   EMAIL ADDRESS: _____

ACADEMIC HISTORY

STUDENT ID: _____
CHALLENGES: _____
STRENGTHS: _____

MEDICAL INFORMATION

PRIMARY CONTACT INFORMATION

EMERGENCY CONTACT INFORMATION

ADDITIONAL INFORMATION

STUDENT *Information*

STUDENT INFORMATION

NAME: _____ BIRTH DATE: _____

ADDRESS: _____ PARENTS NAMES: _____

PHONE: _____ EMAIL ADDRESS: _____

ACADEMIC HISTORY

STUDENT ID: _____

CHALLENGES: _____

STRENGTHS: _____

MEDICAL INFORMATION

PRIMARY CONTACT INFORMATION

EMERGENCY CONTACT INFORMATION

ADDITIONAL INFORMATION

Manufactured by Amazon.ca
Bolton, ON